Easy Grammar® Grade 5
Student Test Booklet

Wanda C. Phillips, Ed.D.

PUBLISHED BY EASY GRAMMAR SYSTEMS INC.

7717 E. Greenway Road

Scottsdale, AZ 85260

www.easygrammar.com

© 2006

TABLE OF CONTENTS

TESTS

Name_____   **PRE-ASSESSMENT**

Date_____

A. Sentence Types:
   Directions: Write the sentence type on the line.

1. _____   You're right!

2. _____   My dog has fleas.

3. _____   Stand in this line.

4. _____   May I have a pear?

B. Sentences, Fragments, and Run-Ons:
   Directions: Write **S** if the words form a sentence. Write **F** if the words
                  form a fragment. Write **R-O** if the words form a run-on.

1. ____   I want a teddy bear my sister wants a stuffed pig.

2. ____   Your juice by the side of the bed warm.

3. ____   Catches the bus each morning at 7 o'clock to go to school early.

4. ____   Do you know today's date?

C. Friendly Letters:
   Directions: Label the parts of this friendly letter:

                                              5 North Drive
   _____   **South Beach, OR   97366**
                                              June 22, 20—

   Dear Terri,   _____

          What are you doing this summer? Did you join a basketball

   team? Have you gone hiking in the hills near your ranch? Are you

   and your family coming to Oregon again this summer? _____

                                      Always, _____
                                      Bo   _____

1

D. Capitalization:
   Directions: Write a capital letter above any word that should be capitalized.

1. bo travels on interstate 65 to diamond caverns near nolin lake state park.

2. "our women's club visited temple sinai on dole street," said dr. jo ming.

3. do mom and i need to buy german chocolate at mayday foods?

4. dear jane,

     did your aunt jenny study english or history at phoenix college
   during the summer she spent in the west?

                                                      your friend,
                                                      jose

5. have you visited cliff house at point lobos near the golden gate bridge?

E. Punctuation:
   Directions: Insert needed punctuation.

1. Hannah was the meeting held on Mon Sept 12 2005 asked Ty

2. Tate said quietly I dont want Johns two toned rusted bike

3. Has Mr Dee your neighbor moved to 2 N Dale Ln Culver City CA 90232

4. Yikes We have to leave at 4 00 and take the following straws ice and
   twenty two cups

5. Yes he read the book entitled Call of the Wild but he hasn't had the oppor
   tunity to read The Raven a poem by E A Poe

F. Subjects and Verbs:
   Directions: Underline the subject once and the verb or verb phrase twice.
   Note: Crossing out prepositional phrases will help you.

1. After the snowstorm, many small children began to play in the snow.

2. One of the pilots stood and greeted passengers at the airport.

3. The doctor and his patient will talk about a pimple under his arm.

4. Stand by the man with the briefcase for a quick snapshot.

2

G. Contractions:
   Directions: Write the contraction.

1. she is - _____   4. I shall - _____   7. who is - _____

2. has not - _____   5. cannot - _____   8. is not - _____

3. I would - _____   6. will not - _____   9. I have - _____

H. You're/Your, It's/Its, and They're/Their/There:
   Directions: Circle the correct word.

1. (There, Their, They're) playing soccer this afternoon.

2. (You're, Your) usually on time.

3. When (its, it's) sunny, they eat (there, their, they're) lunch outside.

I. Subject-Verb Agreement:
   Directions: Underline the subject once. Underline the verb that agrees twice.

1. Chan and his brother (listen, listens) to country music.

2. Her job for social services (seem, seems) like a good one.

3. One of the girls (sleep, sleeps) late.

J. Irregular Verbs:
   Directions: Underline the subject once and the correct verb phrase twice.

1. Peter should have (ran, run) in the first race.

2. Was ice (froze, frozen) on the park's pond?

3. She must have (came, come) alone.

4. Two ladies have (laid, lain) by the pool for an hour.

5. They may have (went, gone) earlier.

6. Some horses had (drunk, drank) their water.

3

K. Tenses:
   Directions: Underline the subject once and the verb or verb phrase twice. Write the tense in the blank.

1. _____ Will you join our team?

2. _____ Water lapped into the canoe.

3. _____ My brothers like to drive to Tulsa.

L. Common and Proper Nouns:
   Directions: Place a ✓ if the noun is common.

1. ____   DOG   2. ____   POODLE   3. ____   FIFI

M. Singular and Plural Nouns:
   Directions: Write the correct spelling of each plural noun.

1. wax - _____   5. bluejay - _____

2. miss - _____   6. torch - _____

3. goose - _____   7. fun - _____

4. puff - _____   8. knife - _____

N. Possessive Nouns:
   Directions: Write the possessive in each blank.

1. dogs owned by his neighbor - _____

2. a closet used by guests - _____

3. tools shared by more than one craftsman - _____

O. Identifying Nouns:
   Directions: Circle any nouns.

1. My idea is to take this shovel, a sleeping bag, two tents, and some strong rope.

4

P. Usage and Knowledge:

1. Write a conjunction: _____

2. Write the antecedent: A crow flapped its wings. _____

3. Write an interjection: _____

4. Write a regular verb: _____

5. Write a linking verb: _____

6. What is the predicate adjective of this sentence? After the first washing, my new blue sweater became fuzzy. _____

7. Write an abstract noun: _____

8. Is the verb action, linking, or neither? The soup <u>tastes</u> spicy. _____

9. Circle the correct answer: I can't see (nobody, anybody) from here.

10. Circle the correct answer: Jacob painted the shed (hisself, himself).

11. Circle the correct answer: Don't walk so (slow, slowly).

12. Circle the correct answer: You played (good, well).

13. Circle the correct answer: I don't feel (good, well).

Q. Identifying Adjectives:
Directions: Circle any adjective.

1. Several tourists visited two old German hotels near a steep, forested region.

R. Degrees of Adjectives:
Directions: Circle the correct answer.

1. That city is (larger, largest) in the state.

2. Jacy becomes (more energetic, most energetic) after exercising.

3. Of the triplets, Faith is (more sensitive, most sensitive).

5

S. Adverbs:
    Directions: Circle any adverbs.

1.   Bo is not usually very late, but he was today.

2.   We are going downtown afterwards.

T.   Degrees of Adverbs:
    Directions: Circle the correct answer.

1.   Marco climbed (higher, highest) on his fifth try.

2.   Of the two birds, the ostrich runs (more swiftly, most swiftly).

3.   She hit the ball (farther, farthest) of the entire team.

U.   Pronouns:
    Directions: Circle the correct answer.

1.   (Me and Roy, Roy and I, Roy and me) looked at a magazine.

2.   Do you want to go with Emma and (I, me)?

3.   We should send (they, them) some maps.

4.   The winner was (she, her).

5.   Our friends and (we, us) will visit Austin next year.

6.   From (who, whom) did you receive your package?

7.   Each of the students must take (his, their) turn.

V.   Nouns and Pronouns Used as Subjects, Direct Objects, Objects of the Preposition, and Predicate Nominatives:
    Directions: Look at the boldfaced word. Write **S.** for subject, **D.O.** for
                 direct object, **O.P.** for object of the preposition, and **P.N.** for
                 predicate nominative.

1. ____   Joe sliced an **apple**.   3.   ____   After swimming, **we** eat a snack.

2. ____   One of the **boys** laughed.   4.   ____   She in the black dress is my **sister**.

6

Directions: Cross out any prepositional phrases. Underline the subject
                once and the verb twice.

1.   My brother lives near a cave in the desert.

2.   A bowling ball rolled slowly down the lane.

3.   The glass beside the sink contains lemonade.

4.   My friend sat at a picnic table under an oak tree.

5.   Their aunt and uncle are from Denver or Dayton.

6.   This book is an essay concerning women during pioneer times.

7.   After the puppet show, they went to a café for lunch.

8.   A tall lady without shoes nodded and walked past me.

9.   Everyone except their mother voted against the bill.

10.   He always stays with his friend until the end of summer.

11.   Ask your parents about their childhood days.

12.   Throughout May, they sit outside their classroom to read.

13.   His grandfather was not in the army before the Korean War.

Name_____   **VERBS**

Date_____   **Test**

A. Directions: Write the contraction.

1. cannot - _____   6. they are - _____

2. he is - _____   7. where is - _____

3. have not - _____   8. is not - _____

4. who is - _____   9. should not - _____

5. did not - _____   10. he will - _____

B. Directions: Circle the correct word.

1. Do you want (they're, their, there) tickets?

2. I'm not sure that (you're, your) on this list.

3. A little chick ran after (it's, its) mother.

4. Most babies coo at (they're, their, there) dads.

5. (It's, Its) good to see you.

6. (They're, Their, There) going to the beach for the weekend.

C. Directions: Underline the subject once and the correct verb phrase twice.

1. This toy is (broke, broken).

2. Snow had (fallen, fell).

3. She must have (driven, drove) alone.

4. Your shirt is (lying, laying) here.

5. Have you (swam, swum) recently?

9

6. The toddler has (blew, blown) bubbles.

7. Models can be (gave, given) the needed information.

8. Nails had been (driven, drove) straight.

9. Ron must have (come, came) late.

10. Have you ever (ran, run) alone?

D. Directions: Circle the correct word.

1. (Sit, Set) your box here.

2. Steam (rose, raised) from the kettle.

3. He must have (lain, laid) his cuff links on the dresser.

4. Are we (setting, sitting) by ourselves?

5. Several old magazines were (lying, laying) beneath an oily rag.

6. The family (rises, raises) money for that charity.

E. Directions: Underline the subject once and the verb or verb phrase twice.
Write the tense (*present*, *past*, or *future*) in the blank.

1. _____ Our kidneys are bean-shaped.

2. _____ Hyenas make a strange sound.

3. _____ Beth suddenly yawned.

4. _____ I shall take your temperature.

5. _____ That fan cheers loudly.

6. _____ Will your friend agree?

10

F. Directions: Underline the subject once and the correct verb twice.

Remember: Crossing out any prepositional phrases helps.

1. My grandmother (deliver, delivers) groceries.

2. I (visits, visit) the Alamo each year.

3. Lana (sips, sip) water through a straw.

4. His mother and Bo (buys, buy) old books.

5. She (don't, doesn't) <u>know</u>.

6. Everyone of his friends (eat, eats) breakfast.

7. Those little girls (giggles, giggle) often.

G. Directions. Cross out any prepositional phrases. Underline the subject once and the verb or verb phrase twice.

1. This mail from Grandpa should be opened now.

2. Deb must have gone without us.

3. The mules stood in the shade and brayed.

4. Can you help me with this necklace?

5. Many blankets were lying on the floor.

6. These gumdrops could be stale.

7. I could not have arrived earlier.

8. You may place your feet here.

9. Each person at the fashion show has received a gift.

10. Does Mike shave and shower every day during the summer?

Name_____ **Cumulative Test**

Date_____ **End of Verb Unit**

Directions: Cross out any prepositional phrases. Underline the subject once
             and the verb or verb phrase twice.

1. Two children without sunblock made sand castles throughout the day.

2. A ball rolled down the sidewalk and into an alley.

3. The man beside me jumped across a pile of boards and plaster.

4. A jacket with red stripes and white stars lay inside the display window.

5. After school, one of the students skipped along a path.

6. The child stood in his crib and cried for his parents.

7. A watercolor by a famous artist hangs over their mantel.

8. The women's club listened to a speech concerning good health.

9. Each person at the fair wanted to ride on the Ferris wheel.

10. A container of small plants has been placed on the window ledge.

11. During intermission, Molly and her sister spoke with the singer's dad.

12. Put this old luggage under the bed.

13. I didn't ask about his trip to Utah.

Name_____   **NOUN TEST**

Date_____

A. Directions: Write **C** in the blank if the noun is concrete and **A** if it is abstract.

1. _____ peace

2. _____ pottery

3. _____ fairness

4. _____ friend

5. _____ daze

6. _____ blister

7. _____ shark

8. _____ fear

B. Directions: Write **C** in the blank if the noun is common and **P** if it is proper.

1. ____ WELDER

2. ____ COLLEGE

3. ____ PLUTO

4. ____ ASIA

5. ____ BULLDOG

6. ____ GARAGE

7. ____ KANSAS

8. ____ STADIUM

C. Directions: Write the plural.

1. cliff - _____

2. apex - _____

3. jersey - _____

4. flea - _____

5. wife - _____

6. gash - _____

7. activity - _____

8. deer - _____

9. fun - _____

10. wrench - _____

11. photo - _____

12. chorus - _____

D. Directions: Write the possessive form in each blank.

1. a business owned by their friend - _____

2. a tearoom belonging to Debra - _____

3. toys shared by more than one child - _____

4. a gift presented by three sisters - _____

5. clients of several companies - _____

E. Directions: Circle any nouns.

Remember: Determiners will help you to find some nouns. You may want to box them in order to help you.

1. Many members of our club are attending that national meeting.

2. Loni's neighbors raise horses on a dude ranch in Wyoming.

3. May Tessa bring her aunt and two cousins to your party?

4. Those sleek boats at this dock are racers with bright stripes.

5. A few students wrote an essay about their trip to Africa during the summer.

F. Directions: Write **S.** if the boldfaced noun serves as a subject.
Write **D.O.** if the boldfaced noun serves as a direct object.
Write **I.O.** if the boldfaced noun serves as an indirect object.
Write **P.N.** if the boldfaced noun serves as a predicate nominative.

1. _____ A guide showed the students a rare **bird**.

2. _____ A **guide** showed the students a rare bird.

3. _____ That rare bird is a bald **eagle**.

4. _____ A guide showed the **students** a rare bird.

16

A. Directions: Cross out any prepositional phrases. Underline the subject once
                 and the verb or verb phrase twice.

1. Several bees buzzed around my head.

2. A bunch of radishes is lying on the ground.

3. Tell us about your trip to Denver.

4. A toothbrush and floss are by the bathroom sink.

5. Several women at the department store chose to buy long coats.

6. I may not come without my sister.

7. Mario walked toward a police officer and waved.

8. We couldn't travel through a tunnel near our home.

9. Joy buys old jewelry from estate sales.

10. A retired athlete sat with his friends and relatives during a game.

11. Many fossils have been found in a cave beyond that cliff.

12. A line of ants scurried around a pebble outside their front door.

B. Directions: Write the contraction.

1. who is - _____   6. I have - _____

2. will not - _____   7. here is - _____

3. are not - _____   8. I am - _____

4. they have - _____   9. could not - _____

5. you will - _____   10. is not - _____

C. Directions: Circle the correct word.

1. (They're, Their, There) toilet bowl has been cleaned.

2. (You're, Your) a good friend.

3. (They're, Their, There) concerned about cavities.

4. A raccoon scampered around (it's, its) dam.

5. Gena wants (your, you're) advice about this program.

D. Directions: Underline the subject once and the correct verb phrase twice.

1. We have (ate, eaten) lunch.

2. He must have (sang, sung) solo.

3. This chain is (broke, broken).

4. I have not (saw, seen) them.

5. Troy may have (taken, took) a trip.

6. Maria had (beat, beaten) his score.

7. Lil has (bought, boughten) soap.

8. The buses have (came, come).

9. She has (driven, drove) her own car.

10. Their dad has (went, gone) alone.

E. Directions: Cross out any prepositional phrases. Underline the subject once and the verb/verb phrase twice. Label any direct object – **D.O.**

1. Jenny drew an arrow across her paper.

2. Since last Thursday, I have earned ten dollars.

3. She carried her checkbook into her bank.

18

F. Directions: Delete any prepositional phrases. Underline the subject once
                  and the verb/verb phrase twice.

1. That club (rises, raises) money for fire victims.

2. Our newspaper was (laying, lying) beside our sidewalk.

3. You may (sit, set) beside us after your performance.

4. I must have (laid, lain) my hammer on the garage floor.

5. The judge (sat, set) his gavel atop her desk.

G. Directions: Underline the subject once and the verb or verb phrase
                  twice. Write the tense (*present, past,* or *future*) in the blank.

1. _____   A feather floated by.

2. _____   Tate enjoys fencing.

3. _____   Tara seemed confused today.

4. _____   Many ducks swim there daily.

5. _____   He will keep a journal.

H. Directions: Delete any prepositional phrases. Underline the subject once.
                  Underline the verb/verb phrase that agrees with the subject twice.

1. Mom often (buy, buys) us treats.

2. A large goose in the gaggle (leads, lead) the others.

3. His dog and cat (chase, chases) each other.

4. Everyone (are, is) in the pool.

5. Tara (does(n't), do(n't)) know me.

6. That man or his wife (run, runs) the business.

7. One of the men (teaches, teach) French.

Name_____   **ADJECTIVES**

Date_____   **Test**

A.   Directions: Circle any adjectives.

1.   Are many large fish in that rushing stream?

2.   One golfer wears a white leather glove with tiny air holes.

3.   A few tourists visited an old railroad office.

4.   The pouring rain ruined their child's paper hat.

5.   White-chocolate brownies are in this gold gift box.

6.   Pam's spacious, modern apartment has no family room.

B.   Directions: Circle any proper adjective. Box any predicate adjective.

1.   Her Eskimo friend is fun-loving.

2.   Our Italian guide seemed pleasant.

3.   A North Sea tour begins tomorrow.

4.   The Chicago skyline is pretty.

C.   Directions: Write the correct degree of adjective.

1.   Your sunglasses are (dark) _____ than mine.

2.   Of the triplets, Kayleigh does (bad) _____ in math.

3.   Their second website is (unusual) _____ than their
      first.

4.   This platinum bracelet is the (expensive) _____
      piece of jewelry in the store.

5.   Of the four forming the new stairway, the top walnut-colored board is (sturdy)

      _____.

A. Directions: Cross out any prepositional phrases. Underline the subject once
                         and the verb or verb phrase twice. Label any direct object – **D.O.**
                         Label any indirect object – **I.O.**

1. A strange noise sounded within the chimney.

2. In the afternoon, those children read and take a nap.

3. A fashion designer and her assistant spoke regarding fabric.

4. Last year, their parents decided to learn about their ancestors.

5. Everyone in the theater applauded after the first act.

6. Use a board without any nails or screws.

7. An English bulldog lay beside a fire in the family room.

8. A hostess handed the laughing customers their menus.

9. Before dawn, we rose and drove to a nearby lake for an outing.

10. Pink asters have been planted near a birdbath.

ॐॐॐॐॐॐॐॐॐॐॐ

B. Directions: Delete any prepositional phrases. Underline the subject once.
                         Underline the verb/verb phrase that agrees with the subject twice.

1. That nurse (takes, take) blood in a laboratory.

2. One of his bosses (want, wants) another computer.

3. Several deputies (patrols, patrol) that area.

4. Their friends (help, helps) during trash pickup.

5. She (does(n't), do(n't)) need a passport.

C. Directions: Write the contraction.

1. did not - _____

2. I have - _____

3. what is - _____

4. you will - _____

5. should not - _____

6. cannot - _____

7. I would - _____

8. I am - _____

9. must not - _____

10. you have - _____

❧❧❧❧❧❧❧❧❧❧❧❧❧

D. Directions: Circle the correct word.

1. (You're, Your) television screen is dusty.

2. (They're, Their, There) must be a better solution.

3. A chicken is roosting in (it's, its) coop.

❧❧❧❧❧❧❧❧❧❧❧❧❧

E. Directions: Underline the subject once and the correct verb phrase twice.

1. One pool player had (brung, brought) his own cue.

2. Have you ever (rode, ridden) an Arabian horse?

3. Moss must have (grown, grew) there.

4. I should have (ate, eaten) breakfast.

5. The producers might have (spoken, spoke) earlier.

6. The crossing guard may have (went, gone) home.

7. Several gliders have (flown, flew) today.

8. She would not have (gave, given) up.

F. Directions: Delete any prepositional phrases. Underline the subject once and the verb/verb phrase twice.

1. You may (lie, lay) on this futon.   4. (Sit, Set) by me.

2. He (rose, raised) his dart.   5. Joy (set, sat) her car alarm.

3. I (laid, lay) my hand over my heart.   6. Bread (rises, raises).

ৰ৹ৰ৹ৰ৹ৰ৹ৰ৹ৰ৹ৰ৹ৰ৹ৰ৹ৰ৹ৰ৹ৰ৹

G. Directions: Underline the subject once and the verb or verb phrase twice. Write the tense (*present, past,* or *future*) in the blank.

1. _____ A security guard latched the door.

2. _____ Chessa and she paint coffee cans.

3. _____ Marco will pay my share.

4. _____ Their lawyer reads real-estate contracts.

5. _____ A yoyo is fun.

ৰ৹ৰ৹ৰ৹ৰ৹ৰ৹ৰ৹ৰ৹ৰ৹ৰ৹ৰ৹ৰ৹ৰ৹

H. Directions: Place a ● if the noun is abstract.

1. ___ CREAM   3. ___ FRIEND   5. ___ PAPERWEIGHT

2. ___ HUNGER   4. ___ FRIENDSHIP   6. ___ DELIGHT

ৰ৹ৰ৹ৰ৹ৰ৹ৰ৹ৰ৹ৰ৹ৰ৹ৰ৹ৰ৹ৰ৹ৰ৹

I. Directions: Place a ⊠ if the noun is proper.

1. ___ MUSTARD   4. ___ DEED   7. ___ BRIAN

2. ___ ALASKA   5. ___ NAPOLEON   8. ___ QUEEN

3. ___ SLUM   6. ___ MT. HOOD   9. ___ JAPAN

25

J. Directions: Write the correct spelling of each plural noun.

1. gurney - _____

2. trout - _____

3. cuff - _____

4. delivery - _____

5. clue - _____

6. chorus - _____

7. flash - _____

8. ox - _____

꙲꙲꙲꙲꙲꙲꙲꙲꙲꙲꙲꙲

K. Directions: Write the possessive form in each blank.

1. a bus belonging to a city - _____

2. books written by more than one child - _____

3. locks created by Vikings - _____

4. guests at a hotel - _____

꙲꙲꙲꙲꙲꙲꙲꙲꙲꙲꙲꙲

L. Directions: Cross out any prepositional phrases. Underline the subject once
                  and the verb twice. Label a predicate nominative – **P.N.** Label a
                  predicate adjective – **P.A.**

1. This problem seems complex.

2. Dakota was a scholarship winner.

3. These pants are too baggy.

4. Their mother became a candidate for governor.

꙲꙲꙲꙲꙲꙲꙲꙲꙲꙲꙲꙲

M. Directions: Circle any nouns.

1. Many billowy clouds blocked the sun from our view.

2. Fran started a job at that employment office last Monday.

26

A. Directions: Circle any adverbs.

1. I do not wash windows well.

2. His little brother hit the ball hard today.

3. Trina leaves her office early on Mondays.

4. They seldom work together on a project.

5. Before the storm, we nailed boards very securely over our windows.

B. Directions: Circle the correct word.

1. My cousin doesn't always clean his room (good, well).

2. The passenger asked the taxi driver to drive (slow, slowly).

3. I like to sing (loud, loudly) in the shower.

4. Stop acting so (weird, weirdly).

C. Directions: Circle the correct degree of adverb.

1. This new motor runs (more smoothly, most smoothly) than the old one.

2. Of the triplets, Emma dances (more beautifully, most beautifully).

3. The doctor answered the patient's second question (more calmly, most calmly).

4. That clerk responds (more helpfully, most helpfully) of all the store's employees.

5. A rodeo rider performed (more skillfully, most skillfully) during the last of the four events.

A. Directions: Cross out any prepositional phrases. Underline the subject once
                  and the verb or verb phrase twice.

1. A tree along the river has fallen against a wooden bridge.

2. After his bath, the baby was bundled and gently dried.

3. Everyone except Todd and Lani stood by a firepit.

ঙ্কঙ্কঙ্কঙ্কঙ্কঙ্কঙ্কঙ্কঙ্কঙ্কঙ্ক

B. Directions: Cross out any prepositional phrases. Underline the subject once
                  and the verb/verb phrase twice. Label any direct object – **D.O.** and
                  any indirect object – **I.O.** Label any object of the preposition – **O.P.**

1. Their sister ordered a video about white-water rafting.

2. Have Nikki and he sold Mrs. Lee logs for her fireplace?

ঙ্কঙ্কঙ্কঙ্কঙ্কঙ্কঙ্কঙ্কঙ্কঙ্কঙ্ক

C. Directions: Delete any prepositional phrases. Underline the subject once.
                  Underline the verb/verb phrase that agrees with the subject twice.

1. Jacy and Ben (hauls, haul) furniture for a moving company.

2. After breakfast, their mom (answers, answer) her email.

3. Those cranes (stay, stays) near the edge of a fish pond.

4. No one in the hotel restaurants (speaks, speak) Spanish.

ঙ্কঙ্কঙ্কঙ্কঙ্কঙ্কঙ্কঙ্কঙ্কঙ্কঙ্ক

D. Directions: Write the contraction.

1. cannot - _____   5. are not - _____   9. I would - _____

2. will not - _____   6. I have - _____   10. she is - _____

3. here is - _____   7. we will - _____   11. they are - _____

4. was not - _____   8. is not - _____   12. I am - _____

E. Directions: Circle the correct word.

1. (They're, Their, There) bird has lost some of (it's, its) tail feathers.

2. I think that (they're, their, there) going to visit (you're, your) aunt.

3. It seems odd that (it's, its) raining (they're, their, there) at this time of year.

ৰৰৰৰৰৰৰৰৰৰৰৰ

F. Directions: Underline the subject once and the correct verb phrase twice.

1. I had (went, gone) early.   5. Has he (brung, brought) his hat?

2. Where have you (rode, ridden)?   6. Kannan has (threw, thrown) a ball.

3. A comet had been (saw, seen).   7. I should have (begun, began) earlier.

4. Snow must have (fell, fallen).   8. Have you (given, gave) blood?

ৰৰৰৰৰৰৰৰৰৰৰৰ

G. Directions: Delete any prepositional phrases. Underline the subject once
                  and the verb/verb phrase twice.

1. Heat (rises, raises).   4. Dad (laid, lay) the mail by his glasses.

2. A box was (laying, lying) nearby. 5. Lani (set, sat) her alarm.

3. He (set, sat) in the back row.   6. I (lay, laid) on a cot for ten minutes.

ৰৰৰৰৰৰৰৰৰৰৰৰ

H. Directions: Underline the subject once and the verb or verb phrase
                  twice. Write the tense (*present, past,* or *future*) in the blank.

1. _____ Barbie sketched a map.

2. _____ Several streams begin here.

3. _____ Jenny will shower soon.

30

I. Directions: Place an **X** if the noun is concrete.

1. ____ CHILI   4. ____ POWER   7. ____ CHALK

2. ____ SOIL   5. ____ JAW   8. ____ IDEA

3. ____ HOPE   6. ____ DOUBT   9. ____ FARM

⋙⋙⋙⋙⋙⋙⋙⋙⋙⋙⋙

J. Directions: Place a ○ if the noun is proper.

1. ____ GENERAL   4. ____ ALBUM   7. ____ LAS VEGAS

2. ____ MASK   5. ____ THANKSGIVING 8. ____ KING

3. ____ ILLINOIS   6. ____ SEA OF CORTEZ 9. ____ BABE RUTH

⋙⋙⋙⋙⋙⋙⋙⋙⋙⋙⋙

K. Directions: Write the correct spelling of each plural noun.

1. faculty - _____   6. organ - _____

2. globe - _____   7. birth - _____

3. halo - _____   8. foot - _____

4. marsh - _____   9. press - _____

5. cliff - _____   10. deer - _____

⋙⋙⋙⋙⋙⋙⋙⋙⋙⋙⋙

L. Directions: Write the possessive form in each blank.

1. visitors to a dude ranch - _____

2. meeting attended by more than one woman - _____

3. buses shared by more than one city - _____

4. a basketball belonging to two girls - _____

M. Directions: Cross out any prepositional phrases. Underline the subject once and the verb twice. Label a predicate nominative – **P.N.** Label a predicate adjective – **P.A.**

1. Her charm bracelet looks silver.

2. A laser is a device with strong light.

3. Their parents were owners of an old mine.

❧❧❧❧❧❧❧❧❧❧❧❧

N. Directions: Circle any nouns.

1. Grammy pulled several onions from the third row of her garden.

2. An orange sign by that old bridge warned people about danger.

❧❧❧❧❧❧❧❧❧❧❧❧

O. Directions: Circle any adjectives.

1. I need four pie crusts and fresh red berries to make an unusual dessert.

2. A few little, frisky puppies played in the Brown's large yard.

❧❧❧❧❧❧❧❧❧❧❧❧

P. Directions: Circle any proper adjective. Box any predicate adjective.

1. Belgian waffles are tasty.

2. Is a grizzly a North American bear?

Q. Directions: Write the correct degree of adjective.

1. That elephant is the (large) _____ animal in our zoo.

2. These red lights are (shiny) _____ than the green ones.

3. The winds during the second storm were (forceful) _____ than during the first.

4. She is the (serious) _____ triplet.

32

Name_____   **PRONOUNS**

Date_____   **Test**

A. Directions: Circle the correct pronoun.

1. My friends and (I, me) are meeting at four o'clock.

2. The new teacher is (he, him) by the copy machine.

3. Do you want to sit between Jim and (I, me).

4. Those girls asked to water the lawn by (themselves, theirselves).

5. Jill doesn't drive (his, her) own car to work.

6. A judge and (she, her) will marry soon.

7. Please allow your brother to do the task (himself, hisself).

8. Some bowlers left (his, their) bowling balls at home.

9. Misty asked (I, me) to help with the prom.

10. For (whom, who) did you buy a present?

11. Our friends agreed with (we, us).

12. Josh and (me, I) made dinner.

13. Will you give (we, us) a donation?

14. Someone left (their, his) sunglasses on the table.

15. (Who, Whom) has washed the dishes?

B   Directions: Circle the possessive pronoun. Write the antecedent in the blank.

1. Did the bee go into its hive?   _____

2. The mechanic finished his test.   _____

3. Patty wanted her mother to wait.   _____

4. A few managers gave their reports. _____   33

A. Directions: Cross out any prepositional phrases. Underline the subject once
                  and the verb or verb phrase twice.

1. In their living room, they placed a hall clock near a bay window.

2. Jose took a deep breath and dived into the water.

3. That jacket with red cuffs is within my price range.

4. During the summer, tugboats and sailboats travel along the coast.

5. An essay concerning New York should be written by Monday.

6. Trim the white border from this poster about rocks.

7. Everyone except Mary crawled through a cave behind the waterfall.

8. During a party at a beach house, some guests walked across the sand.

 споспоспо

B. Directions: Underline the subject once. Underline the verb/verb phrase that
                  agrees with the subject twice.

1. One chef (cook, cooks) delicious gumbo.

2. Their mothers (buys, buy) vintage linens.

3. Mo and his brother (raise, raises) goats.

4. One of the reporters (asks, ask) good questions.

 споспоспо

C. Directions: Write the contraction.

1. cannot - _____   5. do not - _____   9. I would - _____

2. will not - _____   6. I have - _____   10. he is - _____

3. where is - _____   7. we will - _____   11. they are - _____

4. was not - _____   8. is not - _____   12. I am - _____

35

D. Directions: Circle the correct word.

1. If (you're, your) going to the South, visit (they're, their, there).

2. (They're, Their, There) school will hold (it's, its) carnival soon.

3. Do you know if (they're, their, there) hiking near (you're, your) cabin?

ৡৡৡৡৡৡৡৡৡৡৡৡ

E. Directions: Circle the correct verb.

1. He has (went, gone) to the creek.

2. We have (rode, ridden) here alone.

3. My balloon has (busted, burst).

4. I had (saw, seen) him at the store.

5. Has your watch (broken, broke)?

6. One racer has (drove, driven) fast.

7. Have you (brung, brought) water?

8. The horse had (ran, run) far.

9. The sun has (risen, raised).

10. The bell must have (rung, rang).

11. Lou has (ate, eaten) a snack.

12. A patient (laid, lay) on a gurney.

13. She has (given, gave) us a gift.

14. Mike may have (done, did) that.

15. She has (threw, thrown) a curve.

16. I should have (begun, began) early.

17. Our bus had (came, come) late.

18. A dog is (lying, laying) by my door.

ৡৡৡ

F. Directions: Underline the subject once and the verb or verb phrase
twice. Write the tense (*present, past,* or *future*) in the blank.

1. _____ Rough waters scared us.

2. _____ Dad sells cars.

3. _____ The travelers ate tilefish.

4. _____ I like crackers and cheese.

5. _____ Sara will chop wood.

36

G. Directions: Place an **X** if the noun is concrete.

1. ____ chalk   4. ____ faith   7. ____ bickering

2. ____ moss   5. ____ gum   8. ____ pore

3. ____ love   6. ____ weakness   9. ____ flame

掐掐掐

H. Directions: Place a ± if the noun is proper.

1. ____ PLUM ISLAND   4. ____ MT. ETNA   7. ____ COAST

2. ____ LABOR DAY   5. ____ TROUT   8. ____ NANCY

3. ____ PUGET SOUND   6. ____ NEW ENGLAND   9. ____ BOSTON

掐掐掐

I. Directions: Write the correct spelling of each plural noun.

1. omnibus - _____   6. crutch - _____

2. dairy - _____   7. studio - _____

3. virus - _____   8. mouse - _____

4. moose - _____   9. waffle - _____

5. thief - _____   10. reflex - _____

掐掐掐

J. Directions: Write the possessive form in each blank.

1. the doors of our house - _____

2. a bus used by more than one traveler - _____

3. a bird refuge belonging to more than one county - _____

4. a cabin belonging to a captain - _____

5. events planned by more than one woman - _____

37

K.   Directions: Circle any nouns.

1.   The cook and I heated our olive oil in an enamel pan over medium heat.

2.   Many breezes and sounds of the ocean come through the house on that cliff.

၉၇၉၇၉၇

L.   Directions: Circle any adjectives.

1.   A comfortable wicker chair is next to one small trestle table in their dining room.

2. That blonde lady bought hollow, glass vases in several sizes and bright colors.

၉၇၉၇၉၇

M.   Directions: Write the correct degree of adjective.

1.   This new hair dryer is (more powerful, most powerful) than the old one.

2.   Chessa is the (funnier, funniest) student in her class.

3.   We chose the (more colorful, most colorful) poster of the five.

4.   This leather cube is (more durable, most durable) than the sea-grass cube.

၉၇၉၇၉၇

N.   Directions: Circle the correct pronoun.

1.   Mr. Jones gave (we, us) his word.

2.   The winner was (me, I).

3.   Lars and (them, they) drove to a pier.

4.   Take this to Mario and (her, she).

5.   From (whom, who) did you receive the email?

6.   His brother, sisters, and (he, him) should have come in out of the rain.

7.   The girls want to complete the project (themselves, theirselves).

8.   A doorman greeted (us, we) with a huge smile.

9.   Each of the boys must take (his, their) gear to the locker room.

38

O. Directions: Place **X** in the blank if the boldfaced word serves as an adjective.

1. _____ **Several** decided to go.

2. _____ **What** do you know?

3. _____ **This** hut was built last year.

4. _____ With two days' notice, **many** sailors returned to their ship.

5. _____ Cal has decided **which** pogo stick he wants.

෴෴෴

P. Directions: Fill in the blank.

1. Write a possessive pronoun: _____

2. Write an infinitive: _____

3. Write a reflexive pronoun: _____

4. Write an indefinite pronoun: _____

5. What is the antecedent of the possessive pronoun of this sentence?

Lee has taken his dog to a doggie park. _____

෴෴෴

Q. Directions: Circle any adverb.

1. Tessa never goes anywhere alone after dark.

2. One golfer did not score very high yesterday.

3. The couple recently walked downtown together.

෴෴෴

R. Directions: Circle the correct word.

1. I don't feel (well, good).

2. That person always drives (slow, slowly).

3. Stop acting (weirdly, weird) in front of your friends.

S.   Directions: Write the correct degree of adverbs.

1. Tessa skates (smoothly) _____ of anyone in her family.

2. Of the twins, Brian gave his speech (clearly) _____.

3. Ross brushes the mare (briskly) _____ than the colt.

4. At the fourth hole, the golfer hit his ball (hard) _____.

ঌঌঌ

T.   Directions: Look at the boldfaced word in each sentence. Label how it
                   functions in the sentence.

        S. = subject

        P.N. = predicate nominative

        D.O. = direct object

        I.O. = indirect object

        O.P. = object of the preposition

1. _____   Do not scare **me**.

2. _____   His purchase was a **bottle** from India.

3. _____   At the beginning of the day, **Dad** cleaned out our car.

4. _____   The tight end caught the **football** in the end zone.

5. _____   Marco and **she** are rocking on a horse.

6. _____   Ham and eggs were served for **breakfast**.

7. _____   Dee built her **children** a fort in their backyard.

8. _____   The performer received applause for his **acting**.

9. _____   Have you ever seen a **raccoon**?

10. _____   Our uncle is that **man** in the blue and white bulky sweater.

40

Directions: Write the capital letter above any word that needs to be capitalized.

1.   a french explorer brought fruit trees from chile to monterey county.

2.   his uncle, a pilot, entered freeland clinic on east rome street for typhoid

     fever tests.

3.   does grandma montez belong to the carmel stitchers club?

4.   did you eat german sausage at goose creek inn near marina state beach?

5.   dear tate,

          in august, we enjoy the strawberry festival in watsonville, a town in the west.

                                        love always,

                                        tessa

6.   miss lu said, "lee and i attended a craft fair at st. james church on webb lane."

7.   he traveled south on highway 1 to big sur national park on the pacific ocean.

8.   jasmine met me at arlington national cemetery on independence day.

9.   they met general bargas at a republican meeting at bayview cultural center.

10.   has mom read <u>roll of thunder, hear my cry</u> to her reading and english classes?

11.   the arctic circle is south of the brooks range and near the bering sea.

12.   senator jones asked, "have you visited the united nations in new york city?"

13.   in 1864, john freemont proclaimed california to be the bear flag republic.

14.   i studied the louisiana purchase and the trail of tears at wilson college.

Directions: Insert needed punctuation.

1. We wont leave for Boise Idaho until 3 00

2. That boys father is a plumber his mother is a lawyer

3. Dot your i above the letter Anna

4. Dr Heard lives at 802 Robin Drive Orlando Fl 32087

5. Who has read the poem titled Egg Thoughts by R Hoban

6. One woman from a ladies club read the book titled Jamberry to us

7. Jana said I couldnt reach the top shelf

8. They became engaged on Mon February 14 2005

9. Nanny used thirty one shells to make a two colored picture frame

10. Dear Katie

    Yeah We have very exciting news Mandy and Chan our neigh

    bors want to take us to Niagara Falls next summer Do you want

    to come along

                                    Your cousin
                                    Kaylee

11. Dear Judge Minz

12. Yes we need the following a carton of eggs milk and a loaf of bread

13. Mr Wong stayed for a week but he didnt have time to go to an art mu
    seum

14. Mattys mother attended a meeting at the Roth Bldg today said Tate

Name_____   **POST-ASSESSMENT**

Date_____

A. Sentence Types:
    Directions: Write the sentence type on the line.

1. _____   You're right!

2. _____   My dog has fleas.

3. _____   Stand in this line.

4. _____   May I have a pear?

B. Sentences, Fragments, and Run-Ons:
    Directions: Write <u>**S**</u> if the words form a sentence. Write <u>**F**</u> if the words form a fragment. Write <u>**R-O**</u> if the words form a run-on.

1. ____   I want a teddy bear my sister wants a stuffed pig.

2. ____   Your juice by the side of the bed warm.

3. ____   Catches the bus each morning at 7 o'clock to go to school early.

4. ____   Do you know today's date?

C. Friendly Letters:
    Directions: Label the parts of this friendly letter:

                                                     5 North Drive

_____   **South Beach, OR 97366**

                                                     June 22, 20—

Dear Terri,   _____

      What are you doing this summer? Did you join a basketball

team? Have you gone hiking in the hills near your ranch? Are you

and your family coming to Oregon again this summer? _____

                                  Always, _____

                                  Bo   _____

D. Capitalization:
    Directions: Write a capital letter above any word that should be capitalized.

1. bo travels on interstate 65 to diamond caverns near nolin lake state park.

2. "our women's club visited temple sinai on dole street," said dr. jo ming.

3. do mom and i need to buy german chocolate at mayday foods?

4. dear jane,

    did your aunt jenny study english or history at phoenix college
during the summer she spent in the west?
                                your friend,
                                jose

5. have you visited cliff house at point lobos near the golden gate bridge?

E. Punctuation:
    Directions: Insert needed punctuation.

1. Hannah was the meeting held on Mon Sept 12 2005 asked Ty

2. Tate said quietly I dont want Johns two toned rusted bike

3. Has Mr Dee your neighbor moved to 2 N Dale Ln Culver City CA 90232

4. Yikes We have to leave at 4 00 and take the following straws ice and twenty two cups

5. Yes he read the book entitled Call of the Wild but he hasn't had the opportunity to read The Raven a poem by E A Poe

F. Subjects and Verbs:
    Directions: Underline the subject once and the verb or verb phrase twice.
                    Note: Crossing out prepositional phrases will help you.

1. After the snowstorm, many small children began to play in the snow.

2. One of the pilots stood and greeted passengers at the airport.

3. The doctor and his patient will talk about a pimple under his arm.

4. Stand by the man with the briefcase for a quick snapshot.

G. Contractions:
Directions: Write the contraction.

1. she is - _____   4. I shall - _____   7. who is - _____

2. has not - _____   5. cannot - _____   8. is not - _____

3. I would - _____   6. will not - _____   9. I have - _____

H. You're/Your, It's/Its, and They're/Their/There:
Directions: Circle the correct word.

1. (There, Their, They're) playing soccer this afternoon.

2. (You're, Your) usually on time.

3. When (its, it's) sunny, they eat (there, their, they're) lunch outside.

I. Subject-Verb Agreement:
Directions: Underline the subject once. Underline the verb that agrees twice.

1. Chan and his brother (listen, listens) to country music.

2. Her job for social services (seem, seems) like a good one.

3. One of the girls (sleep, sleeps) late.

J. Irregular Verbs:
Directions: Underline the subject once and the correct verb phrase twice.

1. Peter should have (ran, run) in the first race.

2. Was ice (froze, frozen) on the park's pond?

3. She must have (came, come) alone.

4. Two ladies have (laid, lain) by the pool for an hour.

5. They may have (went, gone) earlier.

6. Some horses had (drunk, drank) their water.

K. Tenses:
   Directions: Underline the subject once and the verb or verb phrase twice. Write the tense in the blank.

1. _____ Will you join our team?

2. _____ Water lapped into the canoe.

3. _____ My brothers like to drive to Tulsa.

L. Common and Proper Nouns:
   Directions: Place a ✓ if the noun is common.

1. ____ DOG   2. ____ POODLE   3. ____ FIFI

M. Singular and Plural Nouns:
   Directions: Write the correct spelling of each plural noun.

1. wax - _____   5. bluejay - _____

2. miss - _____   6. torch - _____

3. goose - _____   7. fun - _____

4. puff - _____   8. knife - _____

N. Possessive Nouns:
   Directions: Write the possessive in each blank.

1. dogs owned by his neighbor - _____

2. a closet used by guests - _____

3. tools shared by more than one craftsman - _____

O. Identifying Nouns:
   Directions: Circle any nouns.

1. My idea is to take this shovel, a sleeping bag, two tents, and some strong rope.

48

P. Usage and Knowledge:

1. Write a conjunction: _____

2. Write the antecedent: A crow flapped its wings. _____

3. Write an interjection: _____

4. Write a regular verb: _____

5. Write a linking verb: _____

6. What is the predicate adjective of this sentence? After the first washing, my new blue sweater became fuzzy. _____

7. Write an abstract noun: _____

8. Is the verb action, linking, or neither? The soup <u>tastes</u> spicy. _____

9. Circle the correct answer: I can't see (nobody, anybody) from here.

10. Circle the correct answer: Jacob painted the shed (hisself, himself).

11. Circle the correct answer: Don't walk so (slow, slowly).

12. Circle the correct answer: You played (good, well).

13. Circle the correct answer: I don't feel (good, well).

Q. Identifying Adjectives:
   Directions: Circle any adjective.

1. Several tourists visited two old German hotels near a steep, forested region.

R. Degrees of Adjectives:
   Directions: Circle the correct answer.

1. That city is (larger, largest) in the state.

2. Jacy becomes (more energetic, most energetic) after exercising.

3. Of the triplets, Faith is (more sensitive, most sensitive).

S. Adverbs:
   Directions: Circle any adverbs.

1. Bo is not usually very late, but he was today.

2. We are going downtown afterwards.

T. Degrees of Adverbs:
   Directions: Circle the correct answer.

1. Marco climbed (higher, highest) on his fifth try.

2. Of the two birds, the ostrich runs (more swiftly, most swiftly).

3. She hit the ball (farther, farthest) of the entire team.

U. Pronouns:
   Directions: Circle the correct answer.

1. (Me and Roy, Roy and I, Roy and me) looked at a magazine.

2. Do you want to go with Emma and (I, me)?

3. We should send (they, them) some maps.

4. The winner was (she, her).

5. Our friends and (we, us) will visit Austin next year.

6. From (who, whom) did you receive your package?

7. Each of the students must take (his, their) turn.

V. Nouns and Pronouns Used as Subjects, Direct Objects, Objects of the Preposition, and Predicate Nominatives:
   Directions: Look at the boldfaced word. Write **<u>S.</u>** for subject, **<u>D.O.</u>** for direct object, **<u>O.P.</u>** for object of the preposition, and **<u>P.N.</u>** for predicate nominative.

1. ____ Joe sliced an **apple**.   3. ____ After swimming, **we** eat a snack.

2. ____ One of the **boys** laughed.   4. ____ She in the black dress is my **sister**.